Violin Solo Play-Along with piano,
guitar or violin accompaniment

With a CD of Backing Tracks
and Performances

The Folk Music Fiddler

24 Solos from Around the World
for the Intermediate to Advanced Violinist

Arrangements by Edward Huws Jones

ISBN 978-1-4584-0102-1

BOOSEY & HAWKES

AN IMAGEM COMPANY

DISTRIBUTED BY

HAL•LEONARD®
CORPORATION
7777 W. BLUEMOUND RD. P.O. BOX 13819 MILWAUKEE, WI 53213

www.boosey.com
www.halleonard.com

Notes on the Arrangements

The arrangements in this collection can be performed as solos or duets (or played by larger ensembles), accompanied by piano, violin, or guitar, with or without the CD accompaniment. If the melody is just out of reach, the aspiring fiddler can still join in with the easy violin part. Violinists looking for a challenge can try the violin accompaniment, which powers the ensemble along with incisive rhythms and double-stopped chords.

The printed materials include all the parts you need, and the ensemble sounds on the CD are full of ideas for creating a stylish band with whatever players and resources are available — or for whoever turns up on the night!

Edward Huws Jones

The musical selections included in *The Folk Music Fiddler* have been drawn from the following Edward Huws Jones fiddle collections, published by Boosey & Hawkes:

THE AMERICAN FIDDLER	JAZZ, BLUES, AND RAGTIME
THE CEILIDH COLLECTION	JIGS, REELS, AND HORNPIPES
THE CELTIC FIDDLER	THE KLEZMER FIDDLER
THE FIDDLER PLAYALONG COLLECTION 1	SEVDAH
THE FIDDLER PLAYALONG COLLECTION 2	THE TANGO FIDDLER
THE GYPSY FIDDLER	

Contents

Recording by: CN Productions

Performed by: Frank Mizen (guitar and banjo), Christopher Norton (piano),
John Bone (accordion), Edward Huws Jones (violin)

Blackberry Blossom
AMERICAN

Bluegrass
arranged by Edward Huws Jones

Dusty Miller
AMERICAN

Bluegrass (traditional American)
arranged by Edward Huws Jones

Little Sadie

AMERICAN

Old-time
arranged by Edward Huws Jones

East Tennessee Blues

AMERICAN

Bluegrass (traditional American)
arranged by Edward Huws Jones

De'il among the Tailors
CEILIDH

Reel
arranged by Edward Huws Jones

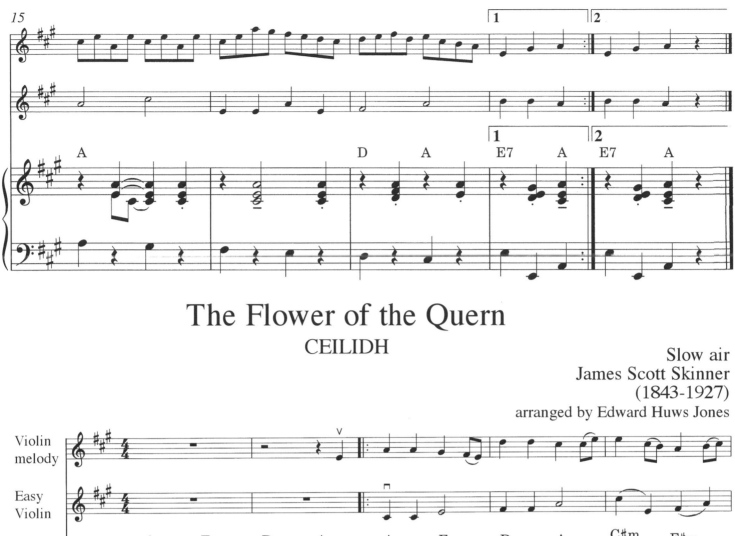

The Flower of the Quern
CEILIDH

Slow air
James Scott Skinner
(1843-1927)
arranged by Edward Huws Jones

Mrs. McLeod's Reel

CEILIDH

Reel
arranged by Edward Huws Jones

Staten Island
CEILIDH

Reel

arranged by Edward Huws Jones

Timour the Tartar
CEILIDH

Reel (traditional Scottish)
arranged by Edward Huws Jones

Go through twice then D. S. to close

Glwysen
The fairest one
CELTIC

Edward Jones
(1752-1824)
arranged by Edward Huws Jones

The Bridge of Saint Paul
Muiñeira: Ponte de San Paio
CELTIC

Traditional Galician
arranged by Edward Huws Jones

The silver leaves of the poplar tree

GYPSY

Traditional Hungarian
arranged by Edward Huws Jones

Song of the Ghetto

GYPSY

Traditional Hungarian
arranged by Edward Huws Jones

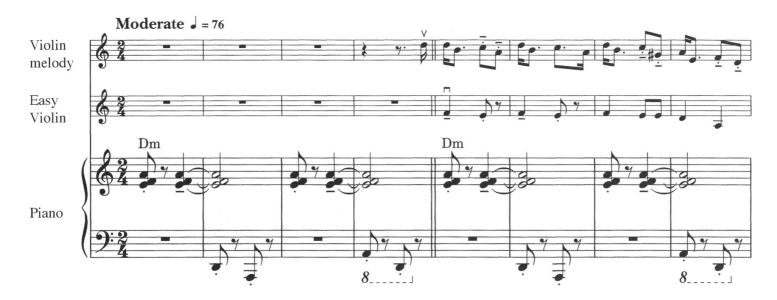

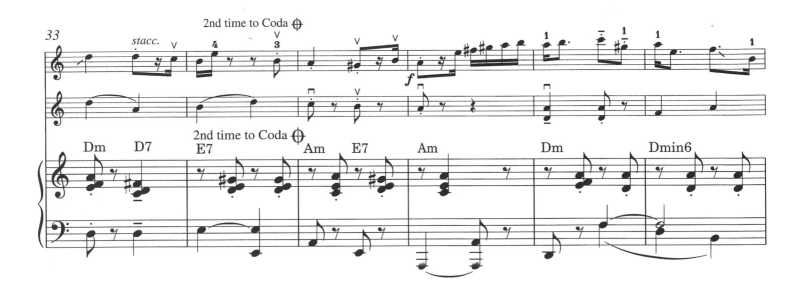

The four corners of my handkerchief

GYPSY

Traditional Hungarian
arranged by Edward Huws Jones

D. C. (slightly faster)

The Bridal
JIGS, REELS, AND HORNPIPES

Jig

arranged by Edward Huws Jones

D.S. al Fine

Carolan's Air
JIGS, REELS, AND HORNPIPES

Turlough O'Carolan
(1670-1738)
arranged by Edward Huws Jones

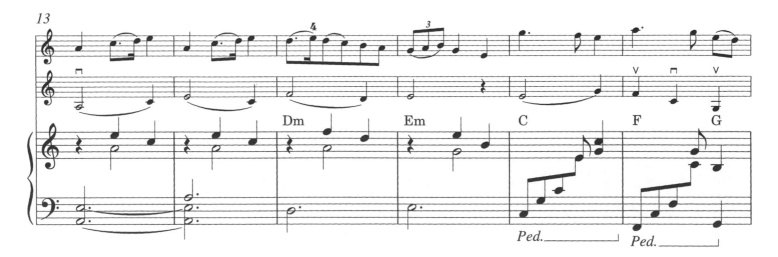

Drowsy Maggie

JIGS, REELS, AND HORNPIPES

Reel (traditional Irish)
arranged by Edward Huws Jones

Red-Haired Boy
JIGS, REELS, AND HORNPIPES

Hornpipe
arranged by Edward Huws Jones

This page intentionally left blank to facilitate page turns.

Dance! Dance!

KLEZMER

Traditional Jewish
arranged by Edward Huws Jones

Freylechs from Warsaw

KLEZMER

Traditional Jewish
arranged by Edward Huws Jones

D. S. al Fine

Paragon Rag
RAGTIME

Scott Joplin
(1868-1917)
arranged by Edward Huws Jones

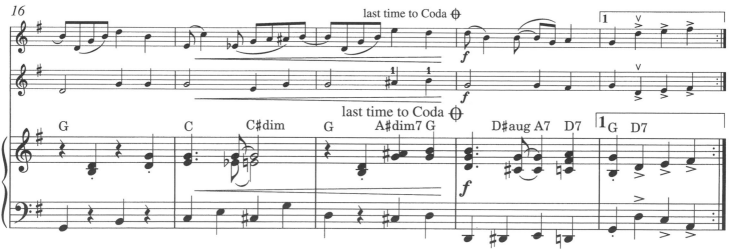

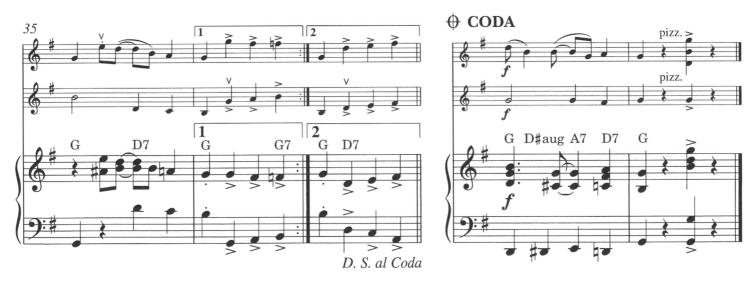

D. S. al Coda

On the Balcony

SEVDAH

Traditional Bosnian
arranged by Edward Huws Jones
and Mehmed Velagíc

El choclo
TANGO

Ángel Villoldo
(1861–1919)
arranged by Edward Huws Jones

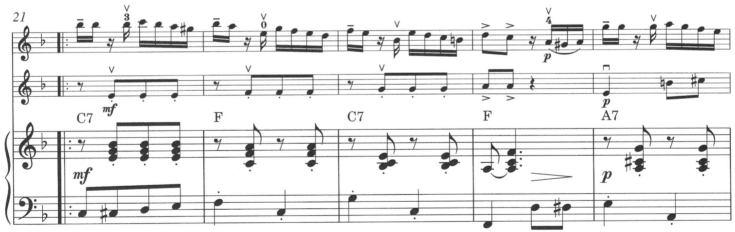

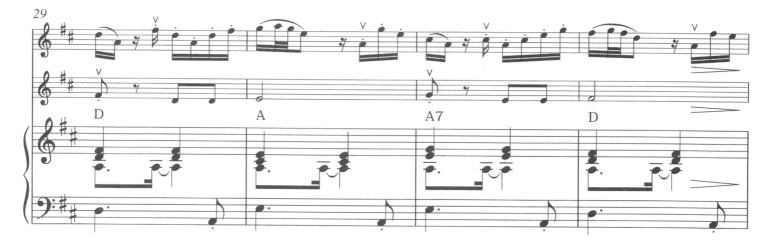

D. S. al Fine

La Cumparsita

TANGO

Gerardo Matos Rodriguez
(1897–1948)
arranged by Edward Huws Jones

TRIO

D. S. al Fine

Other Edward Huws Jones Fiddle Collections

from

BOOSEY & HAWKES

AN IMAGEM COMPANY

THE AMERICAN FIDDLER

26 Old-time, Bluegrass, Cajun, and Texas Style fiddle tunes of the U.S.A. Includes: "Turkey in the Straw," "Cotton-eyed Joe," "East Tennessee Blues," and more.

48011780 Violin and Piano, Complete Edition
48011781 Violin Part

THE CHRISTMAS FIDDLER

15 well-known Christmas fiddle tunes, including "Away in a manger," "Good King Wenceslas," "Silent Night," and more.

48011990 Violin and Piano, Complete Edition
48011991 Violin Part

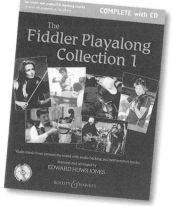

THE CEILIDH COLLECTION

33 traditional fiddle tunes from England, Ireland, and Scotland.

48011621 Violin and Piano, Complete Edition
48011622 Violin Part

THE EARLY MUSIC FIDDLER

20 early music fiddle tunes. Includes Medieval songs and dances, music at court, Renaissance popular music, and the Renaissance dance-band. With notes on each piece.

48012040 Violin and Piano, Complete Edition
48012041 Violin Part

THE CELTIC FIDDLER

30 Celtic fiddle tunes from Ireland, Isle of Man, Galicia, Wales, Brittany, Cornwall, and Scotland.

48012114 Violin and Piano, Complete Edition
48012115 Violin Part

THE FIDDLER PLAYALONG COLLECTION 1

Violin music from around the world with audio backing and performance tracks. Includes 18 selections.

48018957 Violin and Piano, Complete Edition, Book/CD

COMPLETE EDITIONS INCLUDE VIOLIN AND PIANO SCORE,
VIOLIN PART, AND OPTIONAL VIOLIN
ACCOMPANIMENT, EASY VIOLIN AND GUITAR.

THE FIDDLER PLAYALONG COLLECTION VOLUME 2

Building on the success of Volume 1, *The Fiddler Playalong Collection 2* includes 19 selections of violin music from around the world. With audio backing and performance tracks.
48019743 Violin and Piano,
            Complete Edition, Book/CD

THE KLEZMER FIDDLER

Jewish music of celebration. 16 klezmer tunes with performance notes on each piece.
48012031 Violin and Piano, Complete Edition
48012032 Violin Part

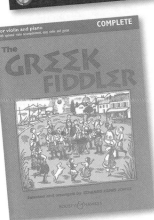

THE GREEK FIDDLER

16 Greek fiddle tunes with notes on each piece.
48019806 Violin and Piano, Complete Edition
48019805 Violin Part

THE LATIN-AMERICAN FIDDLER

12 Latin-American fiddle tunes, including "La bamba," "La cucaracha," "Quizas, quizas, quizas," and more.
48012247 Violin and Piano, Complete Edition
48012248 Violin Part

THE GYPSY FIDDLER

15 Gypsy fiddle tunes from Hungary and Romania. With performance notes.
48011958 Violin and Piano, Complete Edition
48011959 Violin Part

SEVDAH

Traditional music from Bosnia. 10 fiddle tunes with song texts and translations.
48011751 Complete Edition
48011752 Violin Part

JAZZ, BLUES & RAGTIME

12 favorite jazz arrangements for fiddle, including "The Entertainer," "Smoke Gets in Your Eyes," "Tuxedo Junction," and more.
48011516 Violin and Piano, Complete Edition
48011517 Violin Part

THE TANGO FIDDLER

12 tango fiddle tunes, including "El choclo," "La Cumparsita," "Vuelvo al sur," and more. With notes on each piece.
48019240 Violin and Piano, Complete Edition
48019236 Violin Part

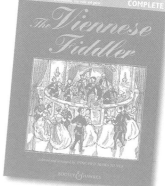

JIGS, REELS & HORNPIPES

30 traditional fiddle tunes from England, Ireland, and Scotland, including "Danny Boy," "Red-Haired Boy," "The Flowers of Edinburgh," and more.
48011347 Violin and Piano, Complete Edition
48011348 Violin Part

THE VIENNESE FIDDLER

12 well-known Viennese violin pieces, including Strauss' "The Beautiful Blue Danube," Suppe's "Light Cavalry," and more.
48012097 Violin and Piano, Complete Edition
48012098 Violin Part

DISTRIBUTED BY

HAL•LEONARD®
CORPORATION

Order from any music retailer, or visit **www.halleonard.com**

About the Enhanced CD

In addition to the performance and backing tracks playable on both your CD player and computer, this enhanced CD also includes tempo adjustment software for computer use only. This software, known as Amazing Slow Downer, was originally created for use in pop music to allow singers and players the freedom to independently adjust both tempo and pitch elements. Because we believe there may be valuable educational use for these features in folk music, we have included this software as a tool for both the teacher and student. For quick and easy installation instructions of this software, please see below.

In recording a backing track we necessarily must choose one tempo. Our choice of tempo, phrasing, ritardandos, and dynamics is carefully considered. But by the nature of recording, it is only one option.

However, we encourage you to explore your own interpretive ideas, which may differ from our recordings. This new software feature allows you to adjust the tempo up and down without affecting the pitch. We recommend that this tempo adjustment feature be used with care and insight.

The audio quality may be somewhat compromised when played through the Amazing Slow Downer. This compromise in quality will not be a factor in playing the CD audio track on a normal CD player or through another audio computer program.

INSTALLATION FROM DOWNLOAD:

For Windows (XP, Vista or 7):
1. Download and save the .zip file to your hard drive.
2. Extract the .zip file.
3. Open the "ASD Lite" folder.
4. Double-click "setup.exe" to run the installer and follow the on-screen instructions.

For Macintosh (OSX 10.4 and up):
1. Download and save the .dmg file to your hard drive.
2. Double-click the .dmg file to mount the "ASD Lite" volume.
3. Double-click the "ASD Lite" volume to see its contents.
4. Drag the "ASD Lite" application into the Application folder.

INSTALLATION FROM CD:

For Windows (XP, Vista or 7):
1. Load the CD-ROM into your CD-ROM drive.
2. Open your CD-ROM drive. You should see a folder named "Amazing Slow Downer." If you only see a list of tracks, you are looking at the audio portion of the disk and most likely do not have a multi-session capable CD-ROM.
3. Open the "Amazing Slow Downer" folder.
4. Double-click "setup.exe" to install the software from the CD-ROM to your hard disk. Follow the on-screen instructions to complete installation.
5. Go to "Start," "Programs" and find the "Amazing Slow Downer Lite" application. Note: To guarantee access to the CD-ROM drive, the user should be logged in as the "Administrator."

For Macintosh (OSX 10.4 or higher):
1. Load the CD-ROM into your CD-ROM drive.
2. Double-click on the data portion of the CD-ROM (which will have the Hal Leonard icon in red and be named as the book).
3. Open the "Amazing OS X" folder.
4. Double-click the "ASD Lite" application icon to run the software from the CD-ROM, or copy this file to your hard drive and run it from there.

MINIMUM SOFTWARE REQUIREMENTS:

For Windows (XP, Vista or 7):
Pentium Processor; Windows XP, Vista, or 7; 8 MB Application RAM; 8x Multi-Session CD-ROM drive

For Macintosh (OS X 10.4 or higher):
Power Macintosh or Intel Processor; Mac OS X 10.4 or higher; MB Application RAM; 8x Multi-Session CD-ROM drive

The Folk Music Fiddler

24 Solos from Around the World
for the Intermediate to Advanced Violinist

Arrangements by Edward Huws Jones

The Easy Violin Part

may be played as an

accompaniment to the

Violin Melody.

ISBN 978-1-4584-0102-1

BOOSEY & HAWKES

AN IMAGEM COMPANY

DISTRIBUTED BY

HAL•LEONARD®
CORPORATION

7777 W. BLUEMOUND RD. P.O. BOX 13819 MILWAUKEE, WI 53213

www.boosey.com
www.halleonard.com

Contents

Recording by: CN Productions

Performed by: Frank Mizen (guitar and banjo), Christopher Norton (piano),
John Bone (accordion), Edward Huws Jones (violin)

Blackberry Blossom
AMERICAN

Bluegrass
arranged by Edward Huws Jones

Dusty Miller
AMERICAN

Bluegrass (traditional American)
arranged by Edward Huws Jones

East Tennessee Blues
AMERICAN

Bluegrass (traditional American)
arranged by Edward Huws Jones

Little Sadie
AMERICAN

Old-time
arranged by Edward Huws Jones

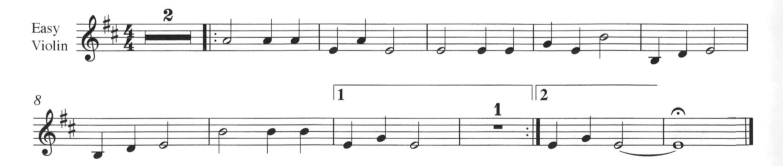

De'il among the Tailors
CEILIDH

Reel
arranged by Edward Huws Jones

The Flower of the Quern
CEILIDH

Slow air
James Scott Skinner
(1843-1927)
arranged by Edward Huws Jones

Mrs. McLeod's Reel
CEILIDH

Reel

arranged by Edward Huws Jones

Staten Island
CEILIDH

Reel
arranged by Edward Huws Jones

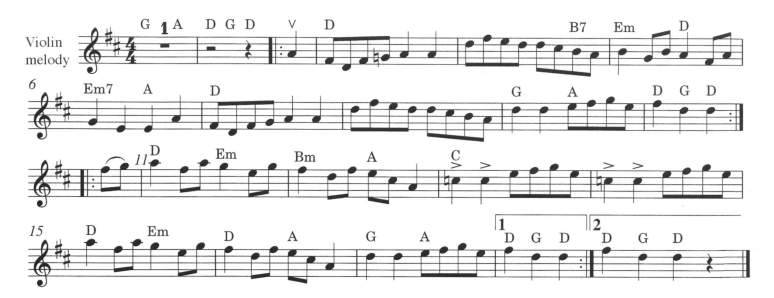

Timour the Tartar
CEILIDH

Reel (traditional Scottish)
arranged by Edward Huws Jones

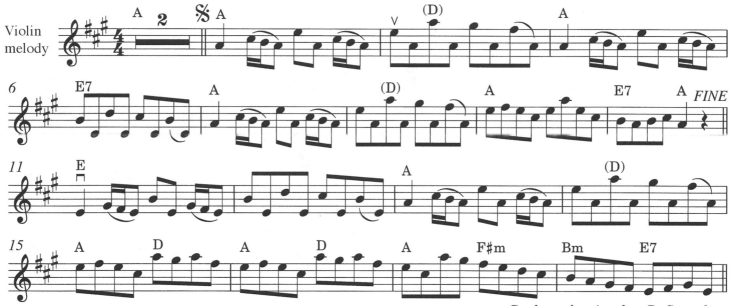

Go through twice then D. S. to close

The Bridge of Saint Paul

Muiñeira: Ponte de San Paio
CELTIC

Traditional Galician
arranged by Edward Huws Jones

Glwysen
The fairest one
CELTIC

Edward Jones
(1752-1824)
arranged by Edward Huws Jones

With feeling

Violin melody

With feeling

Easy Violin

The four corners of my handkerchief

GYPSY

Traditional Hungarian
arranged by Edward Huws Jones

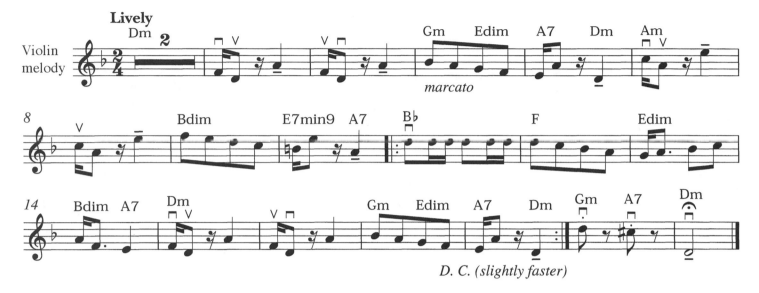

Song of the Ghetto

GYPSY

Traditional Hungarian
arranged by Edward Huws Jones

The silver leaves of the poplar tree
GYPSY

Traditional Hungarian
arranged by Edward Huws Jones

The Bridal
JIGS, REELS, AND HORNPIPES

Jig
arranged by Edward Huws Jones

D. S. al Fine

Carolan's Air
JIGS, REELS, AND HORNPIPES

Turlough O'Carolan
(1670-1738)
arranged by Edward Huws Jones

Drowsy Maggie
JIGS, REELS, AND HORNPIPES

Reel (traditional Irish)
arranged by Edward Huws Jones

Red-Haired Boy
JIGS, REELS, AND HORNPIPES

Hornpipe
arranged by Edward Huws Jones

Dance! Dance!

KLEZMER

Traditional Jewish
arranged by Edward Huws Jones

Not too fast

Violin melody

D. S. al Coda
with repeats

CODA

Not too fast

Easy Violin

D. S. al Coda
with repeats

CODA

Paragon Rag
RAGTIME

Scott Joplin
(1868-1917)
arranged by Edward Huws Jones

On the Balcony

SEVDAH

Traditional Bosnian
arranged by Edward Huws Jones
and Mehmed Velagíc

El choclo
TANGO

Ángel Villoldo
(1861–1919)
arranged by Edward Huws Jones

La Cumparsita

TANGO

Gerardo Matos Rodriguez
(1897–1948)
arranged by Edward Huws Jones

D. S. al Fine

Easy
Violin

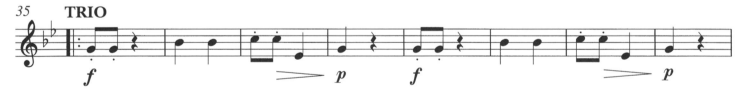

Freylechs from Warsaw

KLEZMER

Traditional Jewish
arranged by Edward Huws Jones

The Folk Music Fiddler

24 Solos from Around the World
for the Intermediate to Advanced Violinist

Arrangements by Edward Huws Jones

ISBN 978-1-4584-0102-1

BOOSEY & HAWKES

AN IMAGEM COMPANY

DISTRIBUTED BY

HAL•LEONARD®
CORPORATION
7777 W. BLUEMOUND RD. P.O. BOX 13819 MILWAUKEE, WI 53213

www.boosey.com
www.halleonard.com

Contents

Recording by: CN Productions

Performed by: Frank Mizen (guitar and banjo), Christopher Norton (piano), John Bone (accordion), Edward Huws Jones (violin)

Blackberry Blossom
AMERICAN

Bluegrass
arranged by Edward Huws Jones

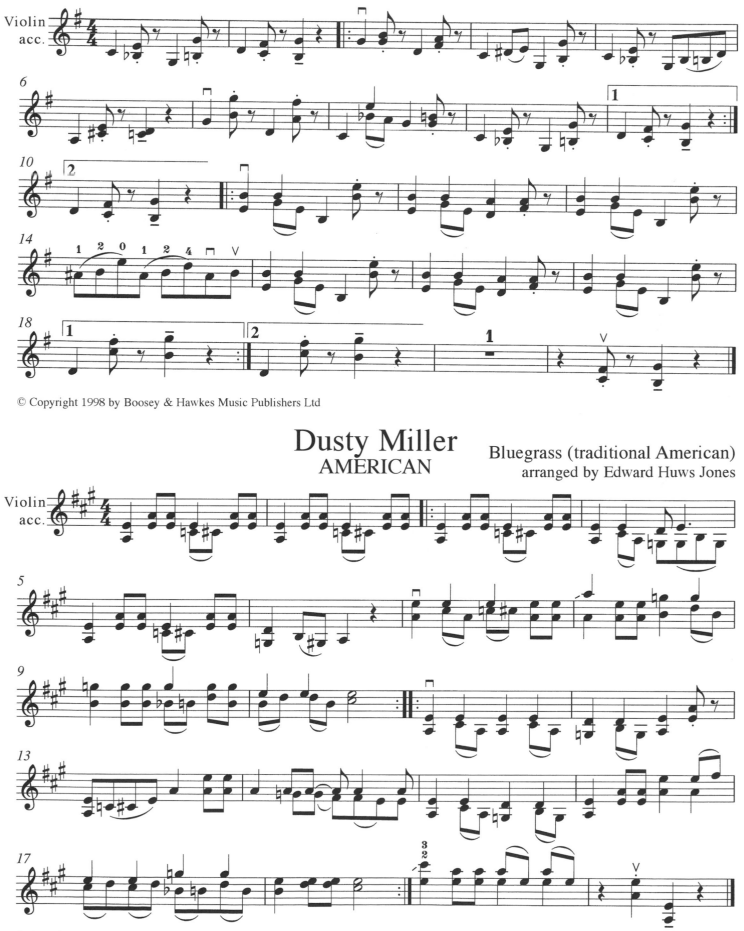

Dusty Miller
AMERICAN

Bluegrass (traditional American)
arranged by Edward Huws Jones

East Tennessee Blues
AMERICAN

Bluegrass (traditional American)
arranged by Edward Huws Jones

Little Sadie
AMERICAN

Old-time
arranged by Edward Huws Jones

The Flower of the Quern
CEILIDH

Slow air
James Scott Skinner
(1843-1927)
arranged by Edward Huws Jones

Mrs. McLeod's Reel
CEILIDH

Reel
arranged by Edward Huws Jones

Staten Island
CEILIDH

Reel
arranged by Edward Huws Jones

Timour the Tartar
CEILIDH

Reel (traditional Scottish)
arranged by Edward Huws Jones

Go through twice then D. S. to close

De'il among the Tailors
CEILIDH

Reel
arranged by Edward Huws Jones

Glwysen
The fairest one
CELTIC

Edward Jones
(1752-1824)
arranged by Edward Huws Jones

With feeling

The Bridge of Saint Paul

Muiñeira: Ponte de San Paio
CELTIC

Traditional Galician
arranged by Edward Huws Jones

The four corners of my handkerchief
GYPSY

Traditional Hungarian
arranged by Edward Huws Jones

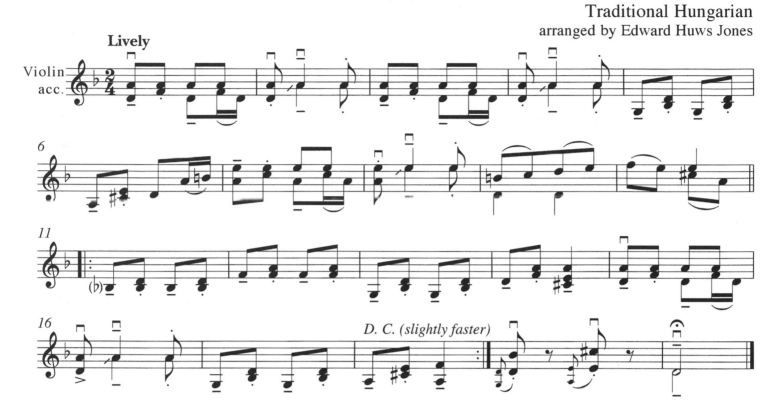

The silver leaves of the poplar tree
GYPSY

Traditional Hungarian
arranged by Edward Huws Jones

Song of the Ghetto

GYPSY

Traditional Hungarian
arranged by Edward Huws Jones

The Bridal
JIGS, REELS, AND HORNPIPES

Jig

arranged by Edward Huws Jones

© Copyright 1992 by Boosey & Hawkes Music Publishers Ltd

Carolan's Air
JIGS, REELS, AND HORNPIPES

Turlough O'Carolan
(1670-1738)

arranged by Edward Huws Jones

© Copyright 1992 by Boosey & Hawkes Music Publishers Ltd

Drowsy Maggie
JIGS, REELS, AND HORNPIPES

Reel (traditional Irish)
arranged by Edward Huws Jones

Red-Haired Boy
JIGS, REELS, AND HORNPIPES

Hornpipe
arranged by Edward Huws Jones

Dance! Dance!
KLEZMER

Traditional Jewish
arranged by Edward Huws Jones

D. S. al Coda
with repeats

Freylechs from Warsaw
KLEZMER

Traditional Jewish
arranged by Edward Huws Jones

Paragon Rag
RAGTIME

Scott Joplin
(1868-1917)
arranged by Edward Huws Jones

D. S. al Coda

On the Balcony

SEVDAH

Traditional Bosnian
arranged by Edward Huws Jones
and Mehmed Velagíc

El choclo
TANGO

Ángel Villoldo
(1861–1919)
arranged by Edward Huws Jones

La Cumparsita

TANGO

Gerardo Matos Rodriguez
(1897–1948)
arranged by Edward Huws Jones

Violin
acc.

D. S. al Fine